# Financial Ratios Explained

# Financial Ratios Explained

*Making Money in the Stock Market*

Matthew T. Williams

**To order additional copies of this book, contact:**
Xlibris Corporation
1-888-795-4274
www.Xlibris.com
Orders@Xlibris.com
54285

# Contents

I would like to dedicate this publication to my younger brother Timothy and younger sister Rachael. I hope you find this book useful for investing.

# Introduction

Well I was going to title this book Financial Ratios Made Easy: Making Money in the Stock Market, but financial ratios are inherently not easy to calculate and to interpret despite all of the books out in the market written on financial statement analysis. The reason why I titled this book as I did, Financial Ratios Explained: Making Money in the Stock Market is because this book attempts to explain the rationale behind the calculations of the many financial ratios that can be used in interpreting financial statements.

The intended audience for this book can be generalized to anyone wanting to know more about performing financial statement analysis though the computation of financial ratios. This book aims not only to explain the calculations of financial ratios, but to aide in the implementation of the use of modern tools such as Excel and online trading to assist potential investors in stock market research and investing.

The overall structure of the book is as follows:

Chapter One will introduce the overall picture of investing, introducing common investment concepts and strategies. In brief, I introduce the reader to my general investing philosophy, and common sense remarks on approaching investing in the stock market.

Chapter Two introduces the reader to the financial statements of a corporation: The Income Statement, Balance Sheet, and Statement of Cash Flows. The intention of this chapter is not to be comprehensive in detailing all of the different line items on the Income Statement, Balance Sheet, and Statement of Cash Flows. In this chapter I introduce the line items that are relevant insofar as being useful for computing financial ratios.

Chapter Three explains the many financial ratios that can be derived from the information contained in the financial statements, and explains the calculations and use of the obtained information. Financial ratios are complex and difficult to calculate correctly. However, in this chapter I explain the calculations in an easy to understand language.

Chapter Four explains how to use Excel to simplify the work that is required to calculate financial ratios. By simply entering information from financial statements of different companies, we can use Excel to calculate these ratios for us. If you follow the step by step instructions in this chapter, you will have a template for using in your independent stock research.

Chapter Five is an overview of two online brokerage services: Ameritrade and E*Trade. Both are great brokerage companies and I have had good experiences with investing in both of these platforms. I give some practical instructions on how to deposit and withdraw money and how to buy and sell stocks.

Chapter Six contains particular stocks that I have researched over the years through financial ratio analysis and gives reasons to why I like those stocks. In this chapter I cover the best twenty two stocks that I have found based on my financial ratio analysis in the past several years or doing research. This chapter will help save the reader from doing these calculations.

Chapter Seven contains information about the Schedule D that will be required to be included in your income taxes if you are selling stocks. I spent two years working for H&R Block and this is just a brief summary of some insights that I gained from reading the IRS publications relevant to investing in stocks.

Chapter Eight explains how we can use Excel to simplify the calculations of short term and long term capital gains for use on the Schedule D. I give several examples of how Excel can be used to track your portfolio returns and to aide in preparing your schedule D.

Chapter Nine is an example of how financial ratios can be used to make an investment decision. In this chapter I juxtapose the Hersey Company and Tootsie Roll and calculate their financial ratios. I integrate the financial ratios into the four categories of liquidity, solvency, profitability, and market measures to come up with the conclusion that the Hersey Company would be a better investment than Tootsie Roll.

Chapter Ten is a bonus chapter that will walk you through using R, a free software package available on the internet that can be used for data and statistical analysis. In this chapter, I use R to create insightful graphs on the stocks that are mentioned in this book. Also, I perform a regression analysis to determine the significant predictors of stock price.

# Chapter One

## My Investment Philosophy

Investing should be easy for almost anyone who has the money to invest in the stock market. Although, it's easy to get burned in the stock market, if you make use of financial ratio analysis, the probability that you will lose money I believe will go down. I have been investing in the stock market since the Fall of 2005 and I have only made money in the stock market. Some of the theories in this book are not meant to be investment advice to anyone; this book is simply an overview of common investment ideas and tools to make the investment process easy. To the extent that I present specific stocks, these are only my opinions on what stocks I would buy and is not to be taken as investment advice.

There are two basic ways of looking for stocks to invest in: fundamental analysis and technical analysis. Although I use both when I am looking for stocks to invest in this book only covers a small portion of what is known about fundamental analysis, i.e. financial ratio analysis. Fundamental analysis is the theory that financial investment decisions are made by looking at the financial statements of a company, and deriving information from those financial statements to choose investments. Whereas, technical analysis is the theory that people should look at the performance of the stock price over time to make investment decisions.

One basic piece of advice that is of common knowledge that I would give is to buy a stock at a low price and sell that stock at a high price. After all the objective of investing in the stock market is to make money right? Buying a stock at a low price may not be that easy since we don't know what direction the stock price will be going, you might object: What if we buy a stock at what seems to be a low price, and then the stock price goes down? My answer to this is to dollar cost average the stocks in your portfolio, i.e. buy the stocks that you are interested in at regular intervals and then the entry points for those stocks will be averaged out.

I think that having six to ten stocks in a portfolio is a good number for being able to track those investments and to make sure that your positions on those stocks don't change. My strategy in investing in the stock market is to buy stocks and to hold them. Although this strategy is not very popular, it's essential for me to keep my costs low, since my portfolio isn't that large. Every time I make a trade it will cost around $13.00. If I decide to change my positions all the time by buying and selling this will eat up my money. Also, another reason to buy and to hold stocks as opposed to "day trading" or buying and selling positions daily is that the IRS makes a distinction between investors and traders. Investors are people who buy and hold stocks for the long term, whereas traders are those people who either buy and sell stocks for a living or who buy and sell stocks frequently.

Based on these principles it's easy to see why I think that investing, and making money in the stock market should be easy for everyone. If you buy stocks that you think are good and buy them at a low price, or dollar cost average them, and then wait for that stock to go up in price, then you will have profits. It's really that easy. This book aims to give you a sense of how I go about picking stocks through fundamental analysis, or by deriving financial ratios from a company's financial statements. I think that this information is useful to anyone who is thinking about investing in the stock market or who is already invested in the stock market.

# Chapter Two

## Financial Statements

What are financial statements and where do they come from? Well, financial statements are basically the report card of a company's financial health. A lot can be learned from looking at the financial statements and there are hundreds of Accounting and Finance books that can explain every piece of the Income Statement, Balance Sheet, and Statement of Cash Flows. I don't go into that kind of detail in this book but if you want to know more just do a Google search. Basically what you need to know about financial statements Is that there are three basic statements that companies make when reporting their numbers to the government: The Income Statement, the Balance Sheet, and the Statement of Cash Flows.

The Income Statement gives information about the income and the expenses of the company and the "bottom line," or the net profit or loss from that business. The Balance Sheet gives information about the assets and liabilities of the company. And, the Statement of Cash Flows shows where the money is coming from and where it's being spent. Financial statements also contain notes and these can be insightful because the management of the company usually presents information about the limitations and potential warning signs for the business and its environment. Financial statements are published by Edgar Online, and can usually be found on the company's website under the investor relations tab. Financial statements are published quarterly and yearly and are also known by the form's names: 10-Q and 10-K, respectively.

For the purposes of this book it's easiest to obtain the financial statement numbers that we are going to use in the calculation of the financial ratios from Yahoo! Finance. I have looked through hundreds of financial statements that I requested directly from the companies that I have researched and have found that the numbers that Yahoo! reports in its finance section are nearly identical to the numbers that the company publishes through their annual reports. If you go to Yahoo! and look up a particular stock symbol for a company that you are interested in, you will find on the left hand side the company's financial statements.

For the purposes of calculating financial ratios, there are only certain line items that are needed from the financial statements. They are listed next with the location of where to find the numbers in the financial statements. Year 1 indicates the year of interest, and Year 2 indicates the year prior to the year of interest.

Sales (Year 1)—Income Statement
Cost of Sales (Year 1)—Income Statement
Depreciation Expense (Year 1)—Statement of Cash Flows
Income before Income Taxes and Interest Expense (Year 1)—Income Statement
Interest Expense (Year 1)—Income Statement
Income before Income Taxes (Year 1)—Income Statement
Taxes (Year 1)—Income Statement
Net Income (Year 1)—Income Statement
Earnings per Share (Year 1)—
Accounts Receivable (Year 1)—Balance Sheet
Accounts Receivable (Year 2)—Balance Sheet
Inventory (Year 1)—Balance Sheet
Inventory (Year 2)—Balance Sheet
Current Assets (Year 1)—Balance Sheet
Current Assets (Year 2)—Balance Sheet
Total Assets (Year 1)—Balance Sheet
Total Assets (Year 2)—Balance Sheet
Current Liabilities (Year 1)—Balance Sheet
Current Liabilities (Year 2)—Balance Sheet
Total Liabilities (Year 1)—Balance Sheet
Total Liabilities (Year 2)—Balance Sheet
Shareholders Equity (Year 1)—Balance Sheet
Shareholders Equity (Year 2)—Balance Sheet
Cash Income from Operations (Year 1)—Statement of Cash Flows
Market Price per Share (Year 1)—Yahoo! Finance

# Chapter Three

## Financial Ratios Explained

Current Ratio

To calculate the Current Ratio, simply divide Current Assets (Year 1) by Current Liabilities (Year 1).

The Current Ratio measures the company's ability to pay for current liabilities from current assets. For example if the Current Ratio is 1, for every dollar in short term debt, the company has 1 dollar in current assets to pay for that debt. The larger the number here, the more assurance we have that the company will be able to pay for its current liabilities from its current assets.

Collection Period

To calculate the collection period, add Accounts Receivables (Year 1) to Accounts Receivables (Year 2) and divide by two. Let's call this number quantity A. Then divide Sales (Year 1) by 365. Let's call this number quantity B. The last step in calculating the Collection Period is to divide quantity A by quantity B.

The Collection Period is the number of days it takes the company to turn its accounts receivables into cash, i.e. the amount of time it takes to collect on its accounts receivables. A lower number indicates that the company has a faster cash flow.

Inventory Turnover

Let's assume that the Cost of Sales (Year 1) is quantity A. Next we need to average the inventory from years 1 and 2. So, simply add Inventory (Year 1) and Inventory (Year 2) and divide by two. Let's call this number quantity

B. The last step in calculating Inventory Turnover is to divide quantity A by quantity B.

Inventory Turnover indicates the number of cycles per year that the inventory turns over, or the number of times that the company sells its inventory.

### Days to Sell Inventory

In order to calculate the Days to Sell Inventory we need to take the average of the inventories in years 1 and 2. So, add Inventory (Year 1) and inventory (Year 2) and divide by two. Let's call this number quantity A. Next, take the Cost of Sales (Year 1) and divide it by 365. Let's call this number quantity B. The last step is to divide quantity A by quantity B.

This final number represents the number of days that the inventory is held prior to being sold.

### Accounts Receivables Turnover

Let's assume that Sales (Year 1) will be called quantity A. Next we need to average the accounts receivables from years 1 and 2. So, add Accounts Receivables (Year 1) and Accounts Receivables (Year 2) and then divide by two. Let's call this quantity B. In order to calculate the Accounts Receivable Turnover, simply divide quantity A by quantity B.

This ratio represents the number of times per year that the accounts receivables are collected. The lower the number here, the longer accounts receivables are being held and the more likely these accounts will go uncollected.

### Current Cash Debt Coverage

Let's assume that the Cash Income from Operations (Year 1) is quantity A. Next we need to average the current liabilities from years 1 and 2. So, add Current Liabilities (Year 1) and Current Liabilities (Year 2) and divide by two. Let's call this number quantity B. The last step in calculating Current Cash Debt Coverage is to divide quantity A by quantity B.

This ratio shows the percentage of debt that current cash flows can pay off.

### Cash Debt Coverage

To calculate the Cash Debt Coverage let's assume that the Cash Income from Operations (Year 1) is quantity A. Next we need to take the sum of the total liabilities from years 1 and 2. So, add Total Liabilities (Year 1) and Total Liabilities (Year 2). Let's call this quantity B. The last step is to divide quantity A by quantity B.

Debt to Total Assets

To calculate Debt to Total Assets, simply divide the Total Liabilities (Year 1) by the Total Assets (Year 1).

Times Interest Earned

To calculate Times Interest Earned, divide Income before Income Taxes and Interest Expense (Year 1) by Interest Expense (Year 1).

The Times Interest Earned ratio represents the extent to which earnings are available to pay off interest payments.

Capital Expenditures

To calculate Capital Expenditures, add Total Assets (Year 1) and Depreciation Expense (Year 1). Then subtract from this number the Total Assets (Year 2).

Capital Expenditures are expenses that are made for the future years' benefit. These expenses cannot be deducted in the year in which they incur; rather, they must be capitalized.

Increase in Net Working Capital

In order to calculate the Increase in Net Working Capital, take Current Assets (Year 1) and subtract Current Liabilities (Year 1). Next subtract from this number Current Assets (Year 2). Finally, add in Current Liabilities (Year 2).

Total Asset Turnover

Let's assume that Sales (Year 1) is quantity A. Next we need to take the average of total assets from years 1 and 2. So, add Total Assets (Year 1) and Total Assets (Year 2) and divide by two. Let's call this number quantity B. Lastly, we divide quantity A by quantity B.

Total Asset Turnover indicates how much revenue is produced from each dollar invested in assets.

Gross Profit Margin Percentage

In order to calculate the Gross Profit Margin Percentage, take Sales (Year 1) and subtract from this number Cost of Sales (Year 1). Next divide the previous number by Sales (Year 1). Finally, multiply the number by 100.

This number represents the percentage of each dollar earned as revenue after subtracting the costs of goods sold.

Operating Profit Margin Percentage

To calculate the Operating Profit Margin Percentage, divide Income before Income Taxes and Interest Expense (Year 1) by Sales (Year 1). Next multiply this number by 100.

Operating Profit Margin Percentage indicates the amount that is made for every dollar in sales before income taxes and interest expense.

Pretax Profit Margin Percentage

To calculate Pretax Profit Margin Percentage divide Income before Income Taxes and Interest Expense (Year 1) by Sales (Year 1). Next, multiply this number by 100.

Pretax Profit Margin Percentage is the amount that the company makes from each 1 dollar in revenue before taxes.

Net Profit Margin Percentage

To calculate the Net Profit Margin Percentage, divide the Net Income (Year 1) by Sales (Year 1). Next, multiply this number by 100.

Net Profit Margin Percentage is the amount of money that the company makes from each 1 dollar in revenue after accounting for taxes and interest expense.

Return on Assets

To calculate Return on Assets, first subtract the Tax Rate (Year 1) from one and multiply this number by the Interest Expense (Year 1). Next add to this number Net Income (Year 1). Let's call this number quantity A. Next we need to take the average of the total assets from years 1 and 2. So, add Total Assets (Year 1) and Total Assets (Year 2) and divide by two. Let's call this number quantity B. Lastly, divide quantity A by quantity B.

Return on Assets is a benchmark for how well management is using the average dollar of the firm's assets.

Return on Common Equity

Let's assume that Net Income (Year 1) is quantity A. Next we need to take the average of shareholders equity for years 1 and 2. So, add Shareholders Equity (Year 1) and Shareholders Equity (Year 2) and divide by two. Let's call this number quantity B. Next divide quantity A by quantity B and multiply this number by 100.

Price to Earnings

The Price to Earnings is calculated by dividing the Market Price per Share (Year 1) by Earnings per Share (Year 1).

Free Cash Flow

In order to calculate Free Cash Flow we need to take Cash Income from Operations (Year 1) and subtract from it the following quantities: Taxes (Year 1), Capital Expenditures, and Increase in Net Working Capital.

# Chapter Four

## Using Excel for Financial Ratios

Excel can be extremely useful in the calculation of financial ratios. If you've never used Excel before, that's okay. This chapter is meant to walk you through the process of creating a template to use for gathering information from financial statements of a company and for computing the financial ratios in Chapter Three. When you first open Excel you will notice that the rows in the spreadsheet are labeled with numbers and the columns in the spreadsheet are labeled with letters. For example A1, represents the cell where row 1 and column A intersect.

Follow these instructions to create your own spreadsheet for calculating the financial ratios in Chapter Three.

Skip cell A1
Skip cell A2
In cell A3 type: Current Ratio
In cell A4 type: Collection Period
In cell A5 type: Inventory Turnover
In cell A6 type: Days to Sell Inventory
In cell A7 type: Accounts Receivables Turnover
In cell A8 type: Current Cash Debt Coverage
In cell A9 type: Cash Debt Coverage
In cell A10 type: Debt to Total Assets
In cell A11 type: Times Interest Earned
In cell A12 type: Free Cash Flow
In cell A13 type: Capital Expenditures
In cell A14 type: Increase in Net Working Capital

In cell A15 type: Total Assets Turnover
In cell A16 type: Gross Profit Margin
In cell A17 type: Operating Profit Margin
In cell A18 type: Pretax Profit Margin
In cell A19 type: Net Profit Margin
In cell A20 type: Return on Assets
In cell A21 type: Return on Common Equity
In cell A22 type: Price to Earnings
Skip cell A23
Skip cell A24
In cell A25 type: Sales (Year 1)
In cell A26 type: Cost of Sales (Year 1)
In cell A27 type: Depreciation Expense (Year 1)
In cell A28 type: Income before Income Taxes and Interest Expense (Year 1)
In cell A29 type: Interest Expense (Year 1)
In cell A30 type: Income before Income Taxes (Year 1)
In cell A31 type: Taxes (Year 1)
In cell A32 type: Tax Rate (Year 1)
In cell A33 type: Net Income (Year 1)
In cell A34 type: Earnings per Share (Year 1)
In cell A35 type: Accounts Receivable (Year 1)
In cell A36 type: Accounts Receivable (Year 2)
In cell A37 type: Inventory (Year 1)
In cell A38 type: Inventory (Year 2)
In cell A39 type: Current Assets (Year 1)
In cell A40 type: Current Assets (Year 2)
In cell A41 type: Total Assets (Year 1)
In cell A42 type: Total Assets (Year 2)
In cell A43 type: Current Liabilities (Year 1)
In cell A44 type: Current Liabilities (Year 2)
In cell A45 type: Total Liabilities (Year 1)
In cell A46 type: Total Liabilities (Year 2)
In cell A47 type: Shareholders Equity (Year 1)
In cell A48 type: Shareholders Equity (Year 2)
In cell A49 type: Cash Income from Operations (Year 1)
In cell A50 type: Market Price per Share (Year 1)

Now let's turn to column B and type in the formulas for calculating the financial ratios. Don't forget to type in the equals sign!

Skip cell B1
Skip cell B2
In cell B3 type:
=B39/B43
In cell B4 type:
=((B35+B36)/2)/(B25/365)
In cell B5 type:
=B26/((B37+B38)/2)
In cell B6 type:
=((B37+B38)/2)/(B26/365)
In cell B7 type:
=B25/((B35+B36)/2)
In cell B8 type:
=B49/((B43+B44)/2)
In cell B9 type:
=B49/(B45+B46)
In cell B10 type:
=B45/B41
In cell B11 type:
=B28/B29
In cell B12 type:
=B49-B31-B13-B14
In cell B13 type:
=B41+B27-B42
In cell B14 type:
=B39-B43-B40+B44
In cell B15 type:
=B25/((B41+B42)/2)
In cell B16 type:
=((B25-B26)/B25)*100
In cell B17 type:
=(B28/B25)*100
In cell B18 type:
=(B30/B25)*100
In cell B19 type:
=(B33/B25)*100
In cell B20 type:
=(B33+B29*(1-B32))/((B41+B42)/2)
In cell B21 type:

=B33/((B47+B48)/2)*100
In cell B22 type:
=B50/B34
In cell B32 type:
=B31/B30

Once all the titles and formulas have been typed in you can begin working with the spreadsheet! The first block of data is where the financial ratios will be calculated by Excel, and the second block of data is where you will enter the information obtained from the financial statements. In Chapter One I outlined the line items that will needed from the financial statements and where to find them. All of these items will be found on the Income Statement, Balance Sheet, or Statement of Cash Flows.

# Chapter Five

## The Ameritrade and E*Trade Platforms

Ameritrade
    To deposit or to withdraw money follow the instructions below:

1.  Click on Portfolios & Accounts from the top toolbar
2.  Click on Deposit/Withdraw from the dropdown sub menu
3.  Select the transaction radio button: Deposit or Withdraw
4.  Enter the withdraw source
5.  Enter the transaction date
6.  Enter the amount

To buy stocks follow the instructions below:

1.  Click Trade from the top toolbar
2.  Click on Stocks from the dropdown sub menu
3.  Select the Buy radio button
4.  Enter the quantity of the stock you want to buy
5.  Enter the symbol of the stock you want to buy
6.  Order type Limit, says that there will be a limit on the amount you are willing to pay
7.  Enter the price you are willing to pay, usually the closing price of the stock on the previous day, or the most recent price on the current day
8.  Expiration is how long you want the order to remain open
9.  Special instructions should be All or None (AON)
10. Routing should be Auto

To sell stocks follow the instructions below:

1. Click on Trade from the top toolbar
2. Click on Stocks from the dropdown sub menu
3. Select the Sell radio button
4. Enter the quantity of the stock that you want to sell
5. Enter the symbol of the stock you want to sell
6. Order type Limit, says that you are willing to receive an amount no less than the price specified
7. Enter the price at which you are willing to sell the stock, usually the closing price of the stock on the previous day, or the current price of the stock on the current day
8. Expiration is the amount of time that you want the order to stay open
9. Special instructions should be All or None (AON)
10. Routing should be Auto

E*Trade

To deposit or to withdraw money follow the instructions below:

1. Click on Accounts from the top toolbar
2. Click on Transfer Money from the sub menu
3. Select the account you want to transfer money from in the dropdown menu
4. Select the account you want to transfer money to in the dropdown menu
5. Enter the amount of money you want to transfer
6. Enter the desired date of the transaction
7. Select the frequency of the transaction from the dropdown menu

To buy or to sell stocks follow the instructions below:

1. Click on Trading & Portfolios from the top menu
2. Click on Trade from the sub menu
3. Select Buy or Sell from the dropdown menu
4. Enter the number of shares that you want to buy or sell
5. Enter the symbol of the stock that you want to buy or sell
6. Select Limit from the Price Type dropdown menu
7. Select the amount of time that you want the order to remain open
8. Click on the All-or-None check box if applicable

# Chapter Six

## Stocks with Good Financial Ratios

The following twenty two stocks are stocks that I have researched and whose financial statements I believe have good financial ratios. The prices that are listed in parentheses are from 9/5/08. I leave the calculation for Earnings per Share to the reader. The amounts for Free Cash Flow, Capital Expenditures, and Increase in Net Working Capital are listed in thousands of dollars. Figures may be rounded.

ACO—*http://www.amcol.com*
Amcol International Corp ($32.30)
2004
Current Ratio = 3.10
Collection Period = 56.66
Inventory Turnover = 6.24
Days to Sell Inventory = 57.72
Accounts Receivable Turnover = 6.35
Current Cash Debt Coverage Ratio = .32
Cash Debt coverage Ratio = .49
Debt to Total Assets Ratio = .06
Times Interest Earned = 43.19
Free Cash Flow = (112090)
Capital Expenditures = 91237
Increase in Net Working Capital = 33553
Total Assets Turnover = 1.53
Gross Profit Margin Percentage = 25.24
Operating Profit Margin Percentage = 7.77

Pretax Profit Margin = 7.64
Net Profit Margin = 6.88
Return on Assets = 10.73
Return on Common Equity = 15.27

ANEN—*http://www.anaren.com*
Anaren Inc ($11.02)
2005
Current Ratio = 8.72
Collection Period = 54.49
Inventory Turnover = 3.59
Days to Sell Inventory = 100.36
Accounts Receivable Turnover = 6.61
Current Cash Debt Coverage Ratio = .70
Cash Debt coverage Ratio = .25
Debt to Total Asset Ratio = .09
Times Interest Earned = 257.67
Free Cash Flow = 55177
Capital Expenditures = (27113)
Increase in Net Working Capital = (21433)
Total Assets Turnover = .49
Gross Profit Margin Percentage = 31.62
Operating Profit Margin Percentage = 8.03
Pretax Profit Margin = 9.69
Net Profit Margin = 7.85
Return on Assets = 3.88
Return on Common Equity = 4.24

CA—*http://www.ca.com*
CA Inc ($22.10)
2005
Current Ratio = 1.08
Collection Period = 79.50
Inventory Turnover =
Days to Sell Inventory =
Accounts Receivable Turnover = 4.53
Current Cash Debt Coverage Ratio = .50
Cash Debt coverage Ratio = .12
Debt to Total Asset Ratio = .56

Times Interest Earned = 1.10
Free Cash Flow = 1194000
Capital Expenditures = 950000
Increase in Net Working Capital = (613000)
Total Assets Turnover = .32
Gross Profit Margin Percentage = 80.91
Operating Profit Margin Percentage = 3.31
Pretax Profit Margin = .31
Net Profit Margin = .31
Return on Assets = 1.25
Return on Common Equity = .23

CL—*http://www.colgate.com*
Colgate Palmolive ($77.07)
2003
Current Ratio = 1.02
Collection Period = 43.04
Inventory Turnover = 6.41
Days to Sell Inventory = 56.15
Accounts Receivable Turnover = 8.37
Current Cash Debt Coverage Ratio = .77
Cash Debt coverage Ratio = .13
Debt to Total Asset Ratio = .88
Times Interest Earned = 17.45
Free Cash Flow = 468300
Capital Expenditures = 707100
Increase in Net Working Capital = (28300)
Total Assets Turnover = 1.36
Gross Profit Margin Percentage = 55
Operating Profit Margin Percentage = 21.87
Pretax Profit Margin = 20.62
Net Profit Margin = 14.35
Return on Assets = 20.70
Return on Common Equity = 229.72

CLDA—*http://www.clda.com*
Clinical Data Inc ($15.94)
2000
Current Ratio = 1.62

Collection Period = 69.62
Inventory Turnover = 3.48
Days to Sell Inventory = 103.52
Accounts Receivable Turnover = 5.17
Current Cash Debt Coverage Ratio = .09
Cash Debt coverage Ratio = .04
Debt to Total Asset Ratio = .52
Times Interest Earned = 5.08
Free Cash Flow = 1356
Capital Expenditures = (962)
Increase in Net Working Capital = (39)
Total Assets Turnover = 1.58
Gross Profit Margin Percentage = 34.06
Operating Profit Margin Percentage = .50
Pretax Profit Margin = 1.20
Net Profit Margin = .76
Return on Assets = 1.31
Return on Common Equity = 2.59

CLX—*http://www.thecloroxcompany.com*
Clorox Co ($62.55)
2005
Current Ratio = .81
Collection Period = 35.73
Inventory Turnover = 7.99
Days to Sell Inventory = 45.05
Accounts Receivable Turnover = 10.08
Current Cash Debt Coverage Ratio = .58
Cash Debt coverage Ratio = .12
Debt to Total Asset Ratio = 1.15
Times Interest Earned = 10.23
Free Cash Flow = 613000
Capital Expenditures = (27000)
Increase in Net Working Capital = (33000)
Total Assets Turnover = 1.18
Gross Profit Margin Percentage = 43.19
Operating Profit Margin Percentage = 18.41
Pretax Profit Margin = 16.61
Net Profit Margin = 24.98

Return on Assets = 30.92
Return on Common Equity = 222.09

COH—*http://www.coach.com*
Coach Inc ($28.60)
2005
Current Ratio = 2.67
Collection Period = 12.75
Inventory Turnover = 2.31
Days to Sell Inventory = 155.98
Accounts Receivable Turnover = 28.24
Current Cash Debt Coverage Ratio = 2.50
Cash Debt coverage Ratio = .94
Debt to Total Asset Ratio = .23
Times Interest Earned = (39.45)
Free Cash Flow = 41000
Capital Expenditures = 360000
Increase in Net Working Capital = (92000)
Total Assets Turnover = 1.43
Gross Profit Margin Percentage = 76.63
Operating Profit Margin Percentage = 36.35
Pretax Profit Margin = 27.28
Net Profit Margin = 22.72
Return on Assets = 31.67
Return on Common Equity = 42.82

CSCO—*http://www.cisco.com*
Cisco Systems Inc ($22.26)
2005
Current Ratio = 2.27
Collection Period = 55.01
Inventory Turnover = 7.30
Days to Sell Inventory = 49.32
Accounts Receivable Turnover = 6.54
Current Cash Debt Coverage Ratio = .76
Cash Debt coverage Ratio = .26
Debt to Total Asset Ratio = .45
Times Interest Earned = (11.57)
Free Cash Flow = (6743000)

Capital Expenditures = 10725000
Increase in Net Working Capital = 1864000
Total Assets Turnover = .74
Gross Profit Margin Percentage = 65.82
Operating Profit Margin Percentage = 24.67
Pretax Profit Margin = 26.80
Net Profit Margin = 19.59
Return on Assets = 13.31
Return on Common Equity = 23.70

HMSY—*http://www.hmsholdings.com*
HMS Holdings Corp ($24.34)
2001
Current Ratio = 2.88
Collection Period = 95.90
Inventory Turnover =
Days to Sell Inventory =
Accounts Receivable Turnover = 3.75
Current Cash Debt Coverage Ratio = (.01)
Cash Debt coverage Ratio =
Debt to Total Asset Ratio = .24
Times Interest Earned = 27.09
Free Cash Flow = 15796
Capital Expenditures = (13046)
Increase in Net Working Capital = (2817)
Total Assets Turnover = .86
Gross Profit Margin Percentage = (30.76)
Operating Profit Margin Percentage = (30.76)
Pretax Profit Margin = (26.89)
Net Profit Margin = (33.13)
Return on Assets = (29.60)
Return on Common Equity = (35.24)

HSY—*http://www.hersheys.com*
Hershey Co ($32.72)
2003
Current Ratio = 1.93
Collection Period = 33.59
Inventory Turnover = 5.11

Days to Sell Inventory = 70.46
Accounts Receivable Turnover = 10.72
Current Cash Debt Coverage Ratio = 1.05
Cash Debt coverage Ratio = .13
Debt to Total Asset Ratio = .64
Times Interest Earned = 12.54
Free Cash Flow = 213525
Capital Expenditures = 282556
Increase in Net Working Capital = (171013)
Total Assets Turnover = 1.18
Gross Profit Margin Percentage = 39.01
Operating Profit Margin Percentage = 19.09
Pretax Profit Margin = 17.56
Net Profit Margin = 10.97
Return on Assets = 14.10
Return on Common Equity = 34.51

INTC—*http://www.intel.com*
Intel Corporation ($20.61)
2004
Current Ratio = 3
Collection Period = 31.35
Inventory Turnover = 5.63
Days to Sell Inventory = 63.97
Accounts Receivable Turnover = 11.48
Current Cash Debt Coverage Ratio = 1.76
Cash Debt coverage Ratio = .70
Debt to Total Asset Ratio = .20
Times Interest Earned = (35.05)
Free Cash Flow = 4579000
Capital Expenditures = 5590000
Increase in Net Working Capital = 49000
Total Assets Turnover = .72
Gross Profit Margin Percentage = 57.72
Operating Profit Margin Percentage = 29.61
Pretax Profit Margin = 30.45
Net Profit Margin = 21.97
Return on Assets = 15.34
Return on Common Equity = 19.67

KMB—*http://www.kimberly-clark.com*
Kimberly-Clark Corp ($62.19)
2004
Current Ratio = 1.09
Collection Period = 47.66
Inventory Turnover = 6.19
Days to Sell Inventory = 58.13
Accounts Receivable Turnover = 7.55
Current Cash Debt Coverage Ratio = .64
Cash Debt coverage Ratio = .13
Debt to Total Asset Ratio = .61
Times Interest Earned = 17.33
Free Cash Flow = 1299000
Capital Expenditures = 1038000
Increase in Net Working Capital = (95000)
Total Assets Turnover = .89
Gross Profit Margin Percentage = 33.60
Operating Profit Margin Percentage = 16.62
Pretax Profit Margin = 14.61
Net Profit Margin = 11.94
Return on Assets = 11.32
Return on Common Equity = 26.88

LDG—*http://www.longs.com*
Longs Drug Stores Corp ($71.81)
2005
Current Ratio = 1.51
Collection Period = 12.59
Inventory Turnover = 7.52
Days to Sell Inventory = 47.90
Accounts Receivable Turnover = 28.59
Current Cash Debt Coverage Ratio = .35
Cash Debt coverage Ratio = .13
Debt to Total Asset Ratio = .48
Times Interest Earned = 5.04
Free Cash Flow = 49000
Capital Expenditures = 48000
Increase in Net Working Capital = 62000
Total Assets Turnover = 3.24

Gross Profit Margin Percentage = 25.75
Operating Profit Margin Percentage = 1.53
Pretax Profit Margin = 1.24
Net Profit Margin = .79
Return on Assets = 3.20
Return on Common Equity = 5.07

LMT—*http://www.lockheedmartin.com*
Lockheed Martin Corporation ($115.72)
2003
Current Ratio = 1.06
Collection Period = 43.52
Inventory Turnover = 12.98
Days to Sell Inventory = 27.73
Accounts Receivable Turnover = 8.27
Current Cash Debt Coverage Ratio = .19
Cash Debt coverage Ratio = .04
Debt to Total Asset Ratio = .74
Times Interest Earned = 4.15
Free Cash Flow = 1951000
Capital Expenditures = (324000)
Increase in Net Working Capital = (297000)
Total Assets Turnover = 1.20
Gross Profit Margin Percentage = 6.21
Operating Profit Margin Percentage = 6.34
Pretax Profit Margin = 4.81
Net Profit Margin = 3.31
Return on Assets = (51.51)
Return on Common Equity = 16.69

MAR—*http://www.marriott.com*
Marriott International Inc ($28.80)
2003
Current Ratio = .70
Collection Period = 24.38
Inventory Turnover =
Days to Sell Inventory =
Accounts Receivable Turnover = 14.76
Current Cash Debt Coverage Ratio = .21

Cash Debt coverage Ratio = .05
Debt to Total Asset Ratio = .53
Times Interest Earned = 3.43
Free Cash Flow = 462000
Capital Expenditures = 41000
Increase in Net Working Capital = (125000)
Total Assets Turnover = 1.09
Gross Profit Margin Percentage = 4.18
Operating Profit Margin Percentage = 4.18
Pretax Profit Margin = 5.41
Net Profit Margin = 5.57
Return on Assets = 7.31
Return on Common Equity = 13.55

MSFT—*http://www.microsoft.com*
Microsoft Corporation ($25.65)
2005
Current Ratio = 2.89
Collection Period = 59.13
Inventory Turnover = 13.60
Days to Sell Inventory = 26.48
Accounts Receivable Turnover = 6.09
Current Cash Debt Coverage Ratio = 1.04
Cash Debt coverage Ratio = .39
Debt to Total Asset Ratio = .32
Times Interest Earned = (6.97)
Free Cash Flow = 58666000
Capital Expenditures = (22698000)
Increase in Net Working Capital = (23737000)
Total Assets Turnover = .48
Gross Profit Margin Percentage = 84.42
Operating Profit Margin Percentage = 36.21
Pretax Profit Margin = 41.79
Net Profit Margin = 30.80
Return on Assets = 12.99
Return on Common Equity = 19.93

OTEX—*http://www.opentext.com*
Open Text Corp ($33.14)

2006
Current Ratio =1.55
Collection Period = 68.98
Inventory Turnover =
Days to Sell Inventory =
Accounts Receivable Turnover = 5.22
Current Cash Debt Coverage Ratio = .39
Cash Debt coverage Ratio = .28
Debt to Total Asset Ratio = .32
Times Interest Earned = (5.49)
Free Cash Flow = (65454)
Capital Expenditures = 69359
Increase in Net Working Capital = 52800
Total Assets Turnover = .62
Gross Profit Margin Percentage = 65.53
Operating Profit Margin Percentage = 1.99
Pretax Profit Margin = 2.36
Net Profit Margin = 1.22
Return on Assets = .63
Return on Common Equity = 1.14

RTN—*http://www.raytheon.com*
Raytheon Co ($59.71)
2003
Current Ratio = 1.71
Collection Period = 11.53
Inventory Turnover = 7.44
Days to Sell Inventory = 48.36
Accounts Receivable Turnover = 31.22
Current Cash Debt Coverage Ratio = .35
Cash Debt coverage Ratio = .05
Debt to Total Asset Ratio = .61
Times Interest Earned = 2.45
Free Cash Flow = 574000
Capital Expenditures = 115000
Increase in Net Working Capital = 653000
Total Assets Turnover = .76
Gross Profit Margin Percentage = 17.17
Operating Profit Margin Percentage = 7.27

Pretax Profit Margin = 4.21
Net Profit Margin = 2.02
Return on Assets = 3.12
Return on Common Equity = 4.05

SKS—*http://www.saksincorporated.com*
Saks Inc ($11.19)
2004
Current Ratio = 2.21
Collection Period = 6.76
Inventory Turnover = 2.70
Days to Sell Inventory = 133.11
Accounts Receivable Turnover = 53.26
Current Cash Debt Coverage Ratio = .38
Cash Debt coverage Ratio = .09
Debt to Total Asset Ratio = .56
Times Interest Earned = 1.70
Free Cash Flow = 27000
Capital Expenditures = 253000
Increase in Net Working Capital = 55000
Total Assets Turnover = 1.37
Gross Profit Margin Percentage = 37.93
Operating Profit Margin Percentage = 5.57
Pretax Profit Margin = 1.31
Net Profit Margin = .95
Return on Assets = 3.06
Return on Common Equity = 2.79

SYY—*http://www.sysco.com*
Sysco Corp ($32.12)
2005
Current Ratio = 1.16
Collection Period = 26.59
Inventory Turnover = 17.07
Days to Sell Inventory = 21.09
Accounts Receivable Turnover = 13.54
Current Cash Debt Coverage Ratio = .36
Cash Debt coverage Ratio = .11
Debt to Total Asset Ratio = .67

Times Interest Earned = 21.34
Free Cash Flow = 71409
Capital Expenditures = 737013
Increase in Net Working Capital = (180561)
Total Assets Turnover = 3.76
Gross Profit Margin Percentage = 19.10
Operating Profit Margin Percentage = 5.29
Pretax Profit Margin = 5.04
Net Profit Margin = 3.18
Return on Assets = 12.52
Return on Common Equity = 36.12

VIVO—*http://www.meridianbioscience.com*
Meridian Bioscience Inc ($25.47)
2004
Current Ratio = 2.17
Collection Period = 74.05
Inventory Turnover = 2.41
Days to Sell Inventory = 149.45
Accounts Receivable Turnover = 4.86
Current Cash Debt Coverage Ratio = .79
Cash Debt coverage Ratio = .17
Debt to Total Asset Ratio = .52
Times Interest Earned = 9.61
Free Cash Flow = 896
Capital Expenditures = 5517
Increase in Net Working Capital = 2230
Total Assets Turnover = 1.17
Gross Profit Margin Percentage = 57.38
Operating Profit Margin Percentage = 18.41
Pretax Profit Margin = 16.58
Net Profit Margin = 11.54
Return on Assets = 15.10
Return on Common Equity = 40.41

WGL—*http://www.wglholdings.com*
WGL Holdings Inc ($31.64)
2004
Current Ratio = 1.05

Collection Period = 25.56
Inventory Turnover = 3.50
Days to Sell Inventory = 102.75
Accounts Receivable Turnover = 14.08
Current Cash Debt Coverage Ratio = .61
Cash Debt coverage Ratio = .08
Debt to Total Asset Ratio = .65
Times Interest Earned = 4.52
Free Cash Flow = 24000
Capital Expenditures = 160000
Increase in Net Working Capital = (3000)
Total Assets Turnover = .85
Gross Profit Margin Percentage = 65.59
Operating Profit Margin Percentage = 9.55
Pretax Profit Margin = 7.59
Net Profit Margin = 4.69
Return on Assets = 5.07
Return on Common Equity = 11.34

# Chapter Seven

## Schedule D

Schedule D is the form that is required by the IRS when engaging in stock sales. Schedule D has two main components: A section for listing short term securities and a section for listing long term securities. A short term sale occurs when you sell a security that has been held for one year or less. A long term sale occurs when a security is sold after holding it for longer than a year. One thing to be aware of is the "wash sale." A wash sale occurs when you sell a security at a loss and you have bought the same security in the previous thirty days, or when you buy the security within 30 days of selling it. I would try to avoid doing this as the tax implications become more complicated in these cases. If you are selling at a gain throughout the year, you may want to make estimated tax payments, to offset the potential taxes that will be owed to the IRS at years end. Another caution is to always try to sell in the same order that you buy stocks. It's required by law that the basis of the stock being sold is calculated starting with the earliest shares acquired.

# Chapter Eight

## Using Excel for Preparing Schedule D

Keeping track of your stock positions is easy to do with Excel. This is a preliminary step in preparing the Schedule D, and will be helpful in tracking your portfolio. Set up the columns in your spreadsheet with the following headings and formulas. Sum each column so that there is a total at the end of each column.

STOCK—Enter the stocks in your portfolio

SHARES—Enter the number of shares of each stock

PRICE—Enter the market price of each stock

POSITION (=SHARES*PRICE)—This formula calculates your position in the stock

PERCENTAGE (=POSITION/TOTAL POSITION*100)—This formula calculates the percentage of each stock that's in your portfolio

COST—Enter the cost of the stock, or what you paid for it plus commissions paid

PERCENTAGE (=COST/TOTAL COST*100)—This formula calculates the percentage of cost that each stock represents

PROFIT (=POSITION-COST)—This formula calculates the profit or loss on each stock

PERCENTAGE (=PROFIT/COST*100)—This formula calculates the percentage of the increase or decrease in the stock relative to its original price, or the return of the stock

Here's an example of this setup:

| | A | B | C | D | E | F | G | H | I |
|---|---|---|---|---|---|---|---|---|---|
| 1 | STOCK | SHARES | PRICE | POSITION | % | COST | % | PROFIT | % |
| 2 | | | | =B2*C2 | =D2/ D7*100 | | =F2/ F7*100 | =D2-F2 | =H2/ F2*100 |
| 3 | | | | =B3*C3 | =D3/ D7*100 | | =F3/ F7*100 | =D3-F3 | =H3/ F3*100 |
| 4 | | | | =B4*C4 | =D4/ D7*100 | | =F4/ F7*100 | =D4-F4 | =H4/ F4*100 |
| 5 | | | | =B5*C5 | =D5/ D7*100 | | =F5/ F7*100 | =D5-F5 | =H5/ F5*100 |
| 6 | | | | =B6*C6 | =D6/ D7*100 | | =F6/ F7*100 | =D6-F6 | =H6/ F6*100 |
| 7 | | | | =sum(D2: D6) | | | | | =H7/ F7*100 |

In order to use Excel for preparing the Schedule D, you have to set up your spreadsheet with the following columns:

DATE BOUGHT—Date the stock was bought

SYMBOL—Symbol of the stock bought

SHARES—Number of shares bought

PRICE—Price at which the stock was bought

COMMISSION—Commission paid on the stock at the time of acquisition

BOUGHT AMOUNT—Total amount paid for the stock plus commission

GAIN/LOSS—SOLD AMOUNT-BOUGHT AMOUNT

SOLD AMOUNT—Amount of money received less the amount paid for commissions for the sale of the stock

DATE SOLD—Date the stock was sold

SHORT TERM OR LONG TERM—Short or long term sale

Here's an example of this setup:

| | A | B | C | D | E | F | G | H | I | J |
|---|---|---|---|---|---|---|---|---|---|---|
| 1 | DATE BOUGHT | SYMBOL | SHARES | PRICE | COMMISSION | BOUGHT AMOUNT | GAIN/ LOSS | SOLD AMOUNT | DATE SOLD | S/L |
| 2 | | | | | | =C2*D2+E2 | =H2-F2 | | | |
| 3 | | | | | | =C3*D3+E3 | =H3-F3 | | | |
| 4 | | | | | | =sum(F2:F3) | =H4-F4 | =sum(H2: H3) | | |

# Chapter Nine

## Comparing Hersey and Tootsie Roll

From calculating the financial ratios of Hershey Foods (HSY) and Tootsie Roll (TR) that measure liquidity, solvency, and profitability I was able to uncover an unbiased comparison of the two company's performances in these areas. In this discussion I will briefly report on the interpretations of the several ratios that were used in each of these three categories. I was able to conclude from this financial analysis that the performance ratios indicate that Tootsie Roll is more liquid and profitable than Hershey Foods. I concluded that Hershey Foods is more solvent than Tootsie Roll based on its superior amount of free cash flow. Although the financial ratios and the underlying company's financial statements indicate that Tootsie Roll has better financial health on two out of three measures analyzed here, I would personally choose and recommend investing in Hershey Foods for its ability to invest in expansion and growth activities. All ratios and comparisons and conclusions are based on 2001 data and are not a current analysis of either company.

Liquidity
From the several computations of ratios that aim to capture liquidity measures, I concluded that Tootsie Roll's financial statements indicate more liquidity than those of Hershey Foods (In this area, Tootsie Roll outperforms Hershey Foods in all of the calculated ratios). In this exercise we want to compute the following ratios that indicate and measure liquidity: Current ratio, collection period, inventory turnover, days to sell inventory, accounts receivable turnover, and current cash debt coverage ratio. On all of these six measures Tootsie Roll's financial statements produced ratios that indicated a superior liquidity factor over those produced by Hershey

Foods' financial statements. Liquidity is important to a company since liquidity is an overall measure of how a company is positioned to convert assets into cash and to obtain cash. Without a superior liquidity factor, a company will not be able to produce the cash for meeting short term obligations. As we have seen in companies with cash flow problems, when short term cash obligations are not being met, then the companies' assets are put at an increased risk and opportunities for discounts and improved profitability become marginal.

The current ratio indicates that since there are more current assets involved per unit of short-term obligations for Tootsie Roll, it will be better able to convert assets into a cash resource, indicating a better short term position in regard to liquidity. The ratio analysis reveals that for every one dollar in currently maturing obligations (short term) there is $4.25 in current assets for Tootsie Roll versus only $1.93 for Hershey Foods. As indicated by the collection rate for receivables, Tootsie Roll is able to collect on its accounts receivables 10 days faster than does Hershey Foods. This will produce a faster cash flow for Tootsie Roll and increases the availability of cash to the company. Inventory measures are also similar in terms of the number of cycles that make it though the company in one year and the average number of days that the inventory exists before it is sold. Tootsie Roll is more efficient in moving the inventory though its cycle at about 5.22 cycles per year vs. 4.77 for Hershey Foods. This efficiency is again reflected in the average days in inventory of 69 days for Tootsie Roll vs. 75.45 days for Hershey Foods. Tootsie Roll's larger A/R turnover ratio of 19.26 indicates that it is more efficient when it comes to issuing credit to its customers and on the matter of collect bad debts. Hershey Foods' low A/R turnover ratio of 12.29 may indicate that a review of credit granting policies and collection practices should be reviewed. The current cash debt coverage ratio indicates that Tootsie Roll is in a slightly better position in producing cash to cover its current liabilities (1.41 vs. 1.03).

Solvency
Based on the ratios that were calculated for determining relative solvency of the two companies, I found that Hershey Foods is more solvent than Tootsie Roll. The ratios that are computed in this section include: Times interest earned, cash debt coverage ratio, debt to total asset ratio, and free cash flow. Solvency is an important measure since it measures a company's capital structure and the firm's ability to meet long term fixed expenses and

to expand for future growth. When a company becomes insolvent, it can no longer meet its long term fixed obligations and it is undergoing bankruptcy. Although Tootsie Roll leads in all of these financial ratios excluding the amount of free cash flow, I decided that this single measure poses a great competitive advantage for Hershey Foods and a very likely detriment to the operational abilities of Tootsie Roll, to meet its long term obligations as well as to engage in expansion and growth activities.

Tootsie Roll is more solvent based on these computations, with the exception of free cash flow, where Hershey Foods is far more superior. Hershey Foods free cash flow is far more superior to that of Tootsie Roll, which puts it in a better financial position for cash generation and its ability to meet its long term fixed obligations as well as to participate in expansion and growth activities. Hershey Foods has a $547 M free cash flow compared to negative $69 M in free cash flow for Tootsie Roll. Assuming that this trend will continue, Hershey Foods will be able to invest in expansion and growth activities, whereas Tootsie Roll will encounter resistance in its attempts for future expansion and growth. In other measures of solvency, Tootsie Roll shows it superiority in the ratio times-interest earned, where Tootsie Rolls' earnings are 284 times its fixed commitments vs. 5.97 for Hershey Foods. The cash debt coverage ratio indicates that Tootsie Roll creates more cash in operating activities to cover total liabilities than Hershey Foods creates through its operations since the cash debt coverage ratio is .38 for Tootsie Roll vs. .16 for Hershey Foods. In the last measure of solvency, debt to total asset ratio, we see that Tootsie Roll finances a lower percentage of its assets through debt. Tootsie Roll finances 18% of its assets though debt vs. 65% of debt financing for Hershey Foods.

Profitability

Overall, I concluded that Tootsie Roll is more profitable than Hershey Foods. The profitability measures that are needed in this analysis include: Gross profit rate, profit margin ratio, return on assets, and asset turnover. I have added another section to this analysis titled Market Measures that will discuss the return on equity and earnings per share of Tootsie Roll and Hershey Foods. Profitability is the measure of intense interest since many believe these ratios to be of paramount importance to a business and its investors and shareholders. Profitability ratios are simply ratio that measure the profitability of the company and are closely related to how a company uses its assets in operating activities.

On the basic profitability measures, Tootsie roll has ratios that indicate a better profitability. For example, the operating profit margin and gross profit margin are both better for Tootsie Roll than they are for Hershey Foods. The operating profit margin indicates that Tootsie Roll is keeping approximately 23.88 % of sales revenue vs. 9.05 % of sales revenue for Hershey Foods at the end of the day. Also, the gross profit margin indicates that Tootsie Roll is more efficient in retaining profits through its manufacturing and distribution processes than the processes at Hershey Foods allow. Tootsie Roll has a gross profit ratio of 48.84 % vs. 41.51 % for Hershey Foods. Both of these ratios indicate that Tootsie Roll is more efficient in retaining profits and suggests that they will be more profitable than Hershey Foods provided that each management team keeps their level of overhead (costs and expenses) at comparable levels.

In regard to the use of assets, Tootsie Roll has a better return on assets, whereas Hershey Foods has a better Asset turnover ratio. For every one dollar invested in assets, Tootsie Roll is able to produce .11 cents in annual earnings prior to subtracting after-tax interest. Hershey Foods is able to convert every dollar in investment monies into .07 cents in earnings prior to after-tax interest. The asset turnover ratio indicates that Hershey Foods has a better ability to generate $1.36 in revenue for every $1 in assets owned, whereas Tootsie Roll is able to generate .72 cents in revenue for every $1 of assets owned, indicating that Hershey Foods generates more revenue from their asset ownership than does Tootsie Roll.

Market Measures

The return on equity for Hershey Foods is higher than that of Tootsie Roll, whereas the price per earnings per share is higher for Tootsie Roll. This may sound contradictory; however, this result is possible since the return on equity ratio is based on the financial statements and there is a market element in the market price in the price per earnings per share ratio. The return on equity for Hershey Foods indicates that for every $1 in equity that is invested, revenue of $17.84 is produced. For Tootsie Roll, every $1 in equity that is invested results in $13.58 in revenues. Despite the efficient use of equity by Hershey Foods, investors are willing to pay proportionately more in order to own a share of Tootsie Roll common stock. The price per earnings per share ratio indicates that in the market, investors are willing to pay $26.87 for every dollar in earnings in the company, vs. just $20.83 for a share in Hershey Foods.

Investment Recommendation

In conclusion of this financial analysis of ratios, Tootsie Roll's financial statements yield better liquidity ratios on all of the ratios computed, and a better measure of overall profitability. Hershey Foods is a clear winner in having financial statements that yield a better picture for solvency, with the computation of the free cash flow as the protruding example. This discussion is very insightful when we combine the financial statement ratios along with the market information in producing an investment recommendation. In the year of 2001, Hershey Foods' stock price rose from $25.15 in the beginning of the year to close at $30.60, producing a 21.67 % increase in 2001. On the other hand, Tootsie Roll's stock price plummeted from an opening price of $37.41 in the beginning of the year to $34.93 at the end of the year, producing a 6.63 % decrease in stock price. Since the end of the year 2001 there has been a 52.29 % increase in the stock price of Hershey Foods to the present day closing price of $46.60, compared to a 14.11 % decrease in the stock price of Tootsie Roll to the present day closing price of $30.00.

Based on the overall content of this analysis, one can make the general conclusion that measures of solvency are dominating the determination of the market price of a stock, since we have concluded that this is the one area where Hershey Foods clearly outperforms Tootsie Roll. This conclusion makes sense to me since the market is composed of institutional and individual investors, who will take into large consideration the solvency measures of a company, when buying a stock. The on-going concern of a company seems to play a critical role of evaluating whether a company's performance warrants the purchase of its stock, even taking precedence over the profitability measures (after all it will not matter whether one company is more profitable than the second if the first company fails to exist in the future). The stock of Hershey Foods presents a much better investing opportunity than does Tootsie roll based on a very general technical analysis. But, in this case a fundamental/ quantitative analysis will also yield the recommendation to by HSY over TR, if the proper weight is assigned to solvency measures.

## Hershey's Stock Prices

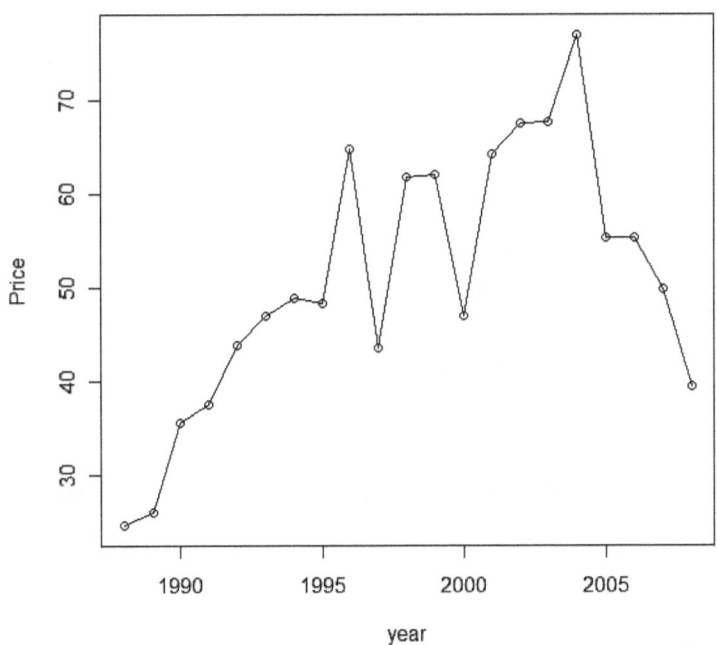

## Tootsie Roll's Stock Prices

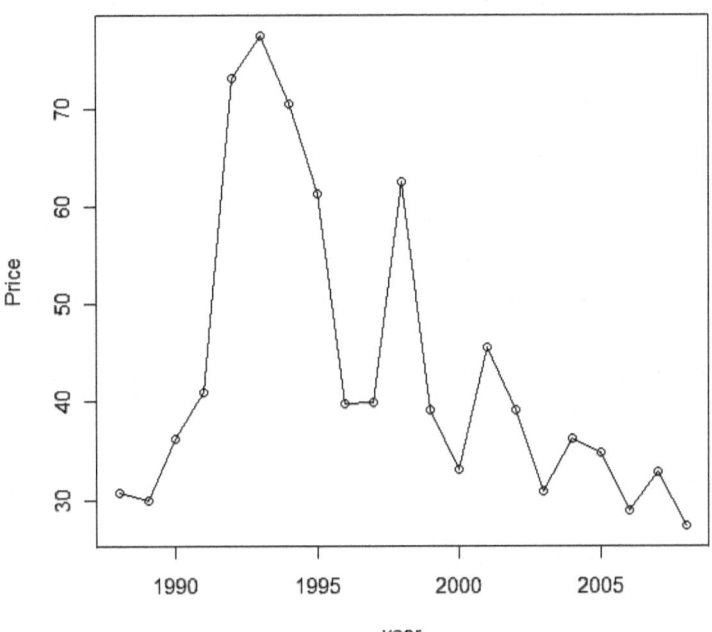

# Chapter Ten

## Using R for Regression Analysis

R is a free software platform available for statistical data analysis. It's available for download at the following website for free (download version R-2.7.1-win32.exe):

*http://cran.cnr.berkeley.edu/*

To download packages for use in R once you have R open, type in the following commands, or simply download the files directly into the library folder on your computer:

```
>chooseCRANmirror()
>install.packages(c("pkg1", "pkg2"))
```

I stored the financial ratio information for the twenty two stocks that I profiled in this book as a .csv file from Excel as frdata.csv. The following codes, graphs, and statistical analysis will attempt to identify those financial characteristics and ratios that are good indicators of stock price. I made an assumption of using the first day of the year following the year in which I gathered information regarding these companies. For example, if the company's year end was sometime in 2003, the year for which I gathered the data, I used the company's stock price on January 1, 2004 for this dataset.

```
>frdata <—read.csv("frdata.csv")
>attach(frdata)
```

The pairs function shows several plots at once and you can get an idea of what relationships exist, if any, between different variable sets.

>pairs(frdata)

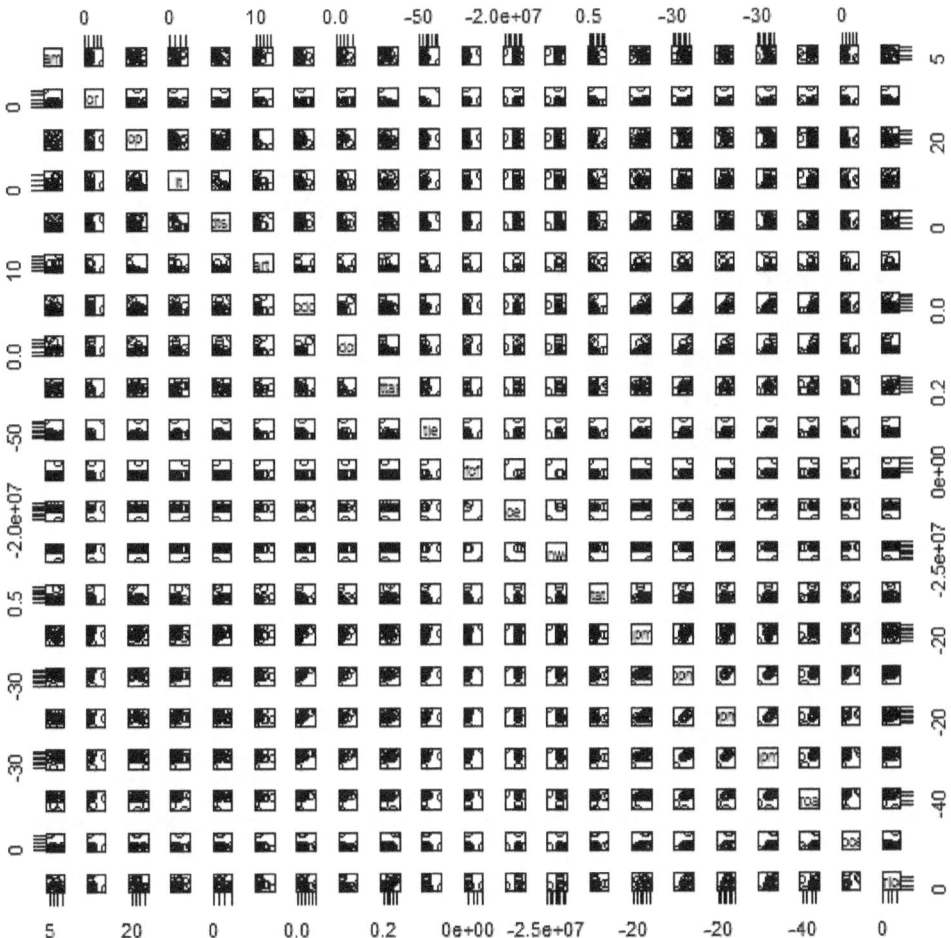

The tree function in R can give us an idea of the distinct groupings that can be made in the dataset. Also, it will give us an idea of what variables might be useful in a linear regression analysis.

```
>require(tree)
>frdatatree <—tree(price ~ .—name, data = frdata, minsize = 1)
>frdatatree
```

```
1) root 22 7.817e+03 31.79
    2) dttar < 0.585 15 1.939e+03 22.40
        4) opm < 1.015 2 5.832e-01 2.73 *
        5) opm > 1.015 13 1.046e+03 25.43
            10) gpm < 10.675 1 0.000e+00 46.08 *
            11) gpm > 10.675 12 5.834e+02 23.70
                22) tie < 7.71 8 3.592e+02 26.69
                    44) tat < 1.4 6 1.600e+02 23.83
                        88) opm < 3.165 2 1.613e+01 17.47 *
                        89) opm > 3.165 4 2.241e+01 27.02 *
                    45) tat > 1.4 2 3.645e+00 35.25 *
                23) tie > 7.71 4 1.073e+01 17.74 *
    3) dttar > 0.585 7 1.724e+03 51.90
        6) art < 12.13 5 5.039e+02 60.25
            12) cr < 1.075 3 2.935e+01 52.85 *
            13) cr > 1.075 2 6.351e+01 71.35 *
        7) art > 12.13 2 6.845e-02 31.02 *
```

```
>plot(frdatatree, type="u")
>text(frdatatree)
```

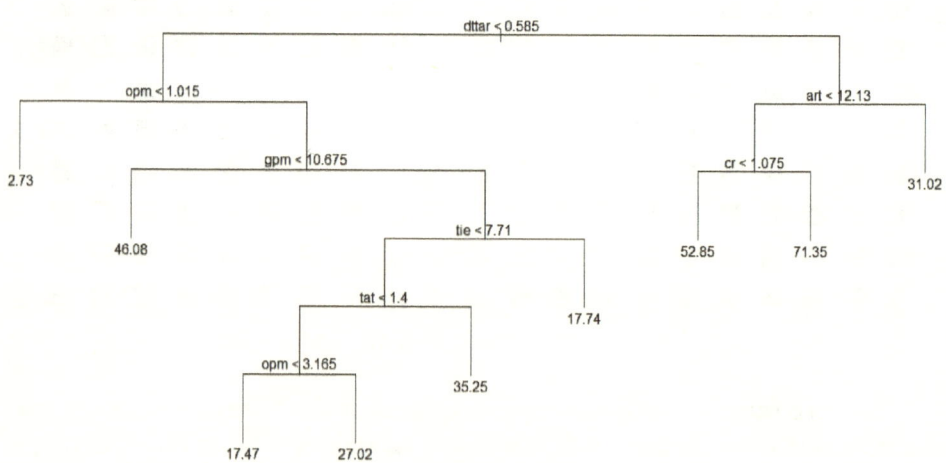

From the regression tree above it can be seen what variables are important in the categorization of this dataset. The following variables are significant in this regression tree:

Debt to Total Asset Ratio
Operating Profit Margin
Gross Profit Margin
Times Interest Earned
Total Assets Turnover
Accounts Receivable Turnover
Current Ratio

Putting this in a linear regression model we get the following:

```
>frdatalm <—lm(price ~ dttar + opm + gpm + tie + tat + art + cr, data
= frdata)
>summary(frdatalm)
```

Call:

```
lm(formula = price ~ dttar + opm + gpm + tie + tat + art + cr,
    data = frdata)
```

Residuals:

```
Min; 1Q; Median; 3Q; Max
-22.504; -5.550; -2.596; 6.978; 32.427
```

Coefficients:

```
Estimate; Std. Error; t value; Pr(>|t|)
(Intercept) 27.58946; 15.5708; 1.772; 0.0982.
dttar 35.49002; 15.93581; 2.227; 0.0429 *
opm 0.91362; 0.34289; 2.664; 0.0185 *
gpm -0.36001; 0.18284; -1.969; 0.0691.
tie 0.05311; 0.09530; 0.557; 0.5861
tat -2.82042; 4.77185; -0.591; 0.5639
art -0.02002; 0.30569; -0.065; 0.9487
cr -3.24376; 3.68923; -0.879; 0.3941
```

———

Signif. codes: 0 '***' 0.001 '**' 0.01 '*' 0.05 '.' 0.1 ' ' 1

Residual standard error: 15.41 on 14 degrees of freedom
Multiple R-squared: 0.5746, Adjusted R-squared: 0.3619
F-statistic: 2.701 on 7 and 14 DF, p-value: 0.05383

Since dttar and opm are significant predictors of price at the alpha = .05 level of significance, let's drop the other variables and see what we get for the final regression model.

```
>frdatalm <- lm(price ~ dttar + opm, data = frdata)
>summary(frdatalm)
```

Call:
    lm(formula = price ~ dttar + opm, data = frdata)

Residuals:
    Min; 1Q; Median; 3Q; Max
    -26.335; -6.568; -1.668; 7.311; 35.918

Coefficients:
    Estimate; Std. Error; t value; Pr(>|t|)
    (Intercept) 5.9792; 7.5293; 0.794; 0.43693
    dttar 42.9745; 12.9953; 3.307; 0.00371 **
    opm 0.3976; 0.2278; 1.745; 0.09716 .
    ⸺
Signif. codes: 0 '***' 0.001 '**' 0.01 '*' 0.05 '.' 0.1 ' ' 1

Residual standard error: 15.23 on 19 degrees of freedom
Multiple R-squared: 0.4362, Adjusted R-squared: 0.3768
F-statistic: 7.349 on 2 and 19 DF, p-value: 0.004324

Now it looks like only dttar is significant, now at the alpha = .001 level of significance. Let's drop opm from the model and see what we get.

```
>frdatalm <- lm(price ~ dttar, data = frdata)
>summary(frdatalm)
```

Call:
    lm(formula = price ~ dttar, data = frdata)

Residuals:
    Min; 1Q; Median; 3Q; Max
    -30.7438; -8.2382; 0.6443; 7.0887; 38.7415

Coefficients:
    Estimate; Std. Error; t value; Pr(>|t|)
    (Intercept) 9.904; 7.544; 1.313; 0.20412
    dttar 44.289; 13.620; 3.252; 0.00400 **

—

    Signif. codes:  0 '***' 0.001 '**' 0.01 '*' 0.05 '.' 0.1 ' ' 1

Residual standard error: 15.99 on 20 degrees of freedom
Multiple R-squared: 0.3458, Adjusted R-squared: 0.3131
F-statistic: 10.57 on 1 and 20 DF, p-value: 0.003996

Here we see that dttar is the significant predictor of stock price. Let's take a closer look at this relationship.

>plot(dttar, price, main = "Relationship Between Price and DTTAR", xlab = "Debt to Total Assets Ratio")

## Relationship Between Price and DTTAR

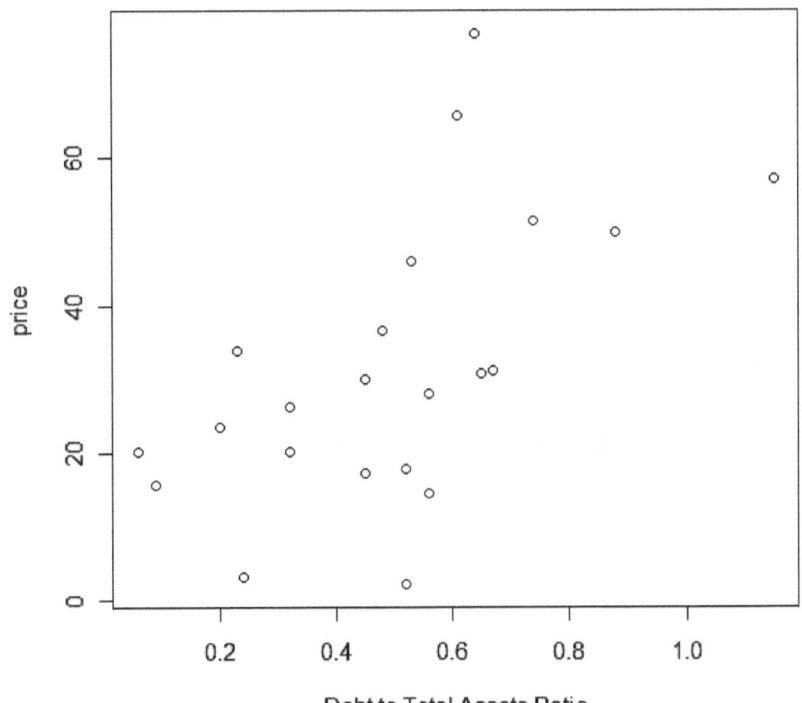

Debt to Total Assets Ratio

Also let's look at the diagnostic plots for this linear regression model. First let's plot the residuals against the predictor Debt to Total Assets Ratio.

>plot(dttar, frdatalm$residuals, main = "Residuals vs. Predictor", xlab = "Debt to Total Assets Ratio", ylab="Residuals")

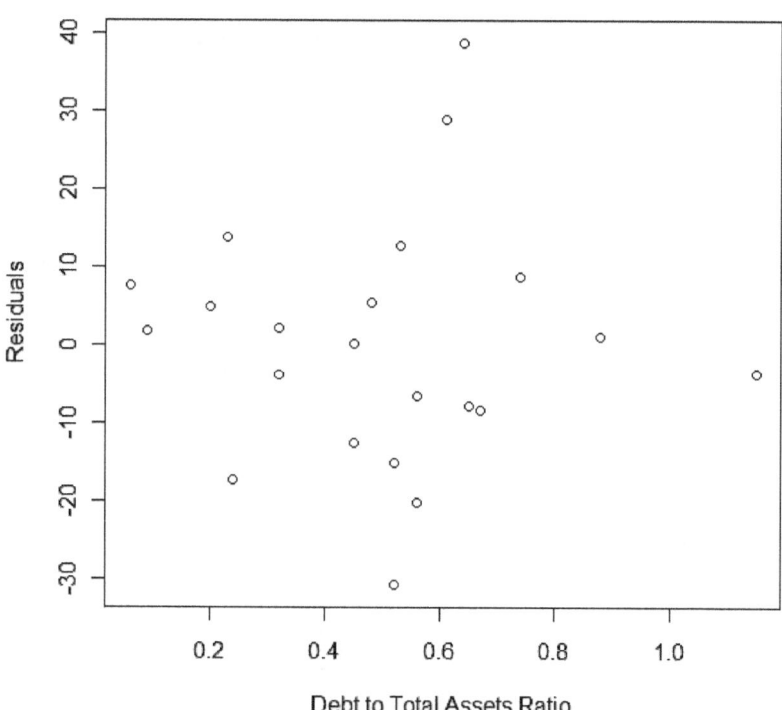

Now let's plot the residuals against the fitted values.

>plot(frdatalm$fitted.values, frdatalm$residuals, main = "Residuals vs. Predictor", xlab = "Fitted Values", ylab = "Residuals")

**Residuals vs. Predictor**

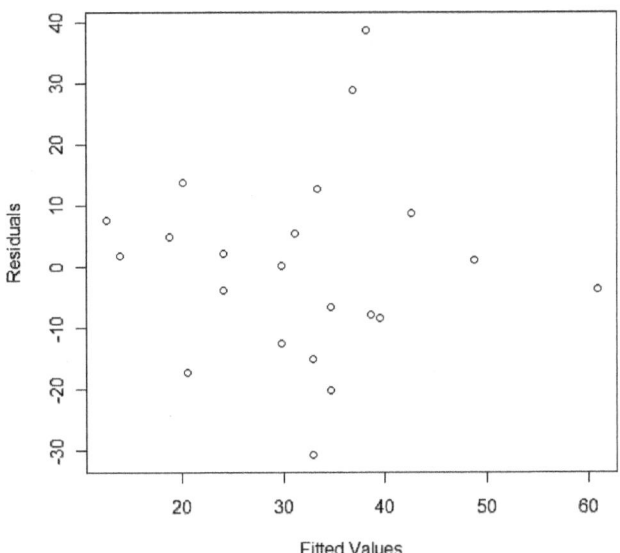

Lastly, let's graph the normal probability plot or the QQ plot.

>qqnorm(frdatalm$residuals, main = "Normal Probability Plot")

**Normal Probability Plot**

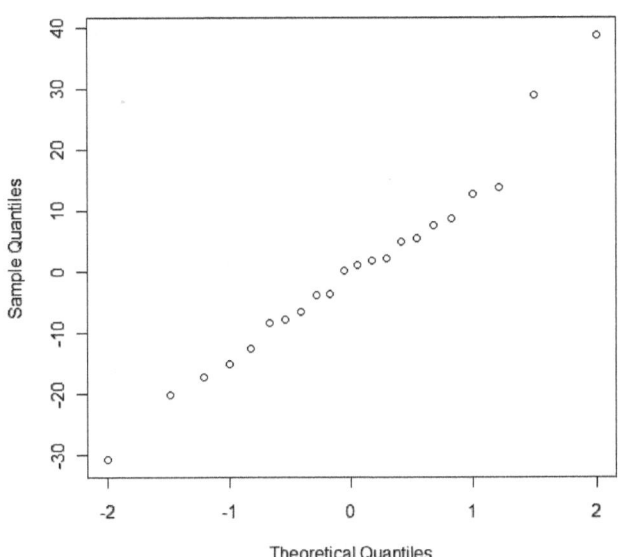

Since all of our assumptions of the linear model hold true it looks like we have a valid model. We can conclude that the regression function is linear, the error terms have constant variance, error terms are independent, and the error terms are normally distributed. Based on our model we can conclude that inside the range of our predictor variable of Debt to Total Asset Ratio, a one unit increment will result in a 44.29 dollar increase in the response variable, price. Y = 9.904 + 44.289 X => Price = 9.904 + 44.289 (Debt to Total Assets Ratio)

# References

Wild, John J. and Subramanyam, K.R. (2003). Financial Statement Analysis. New York: McGraw-Hill Companies.

Shim, Joel G. and Siegel, Jae K. (2005). Dictionary of Accounting Terms. New York: Barron's Educational Series, Inc.